# *THE FREEDOM OF LIFE*

Edited by

Heather Killingray

First published in Great Britain in 2000 by
*POETRY NOW*
Remus House,
Coltsfoot Drive,
Peterborough, PE2 9JX
Telephone (01733) 898101
Fax (01733) 313524



HB ISBN 075432463X
SB ISBN 0754324648

# *FOREWORD*

Although we are a nation of poets we are accused of not reading poetry, or buying poetry books. After many years of listening to the incessant gripes of poetry publishers, I can only assume that the books they publish, in general, are books that most people do not want to read.

Poetry should not be obscure, introverted, and as cryptic as a crossword puzzle: it is the poet's duty to reach out and embrace the world.

The world owes the poet nothing and we should not be expected to dig and delve into a rambling discourse searching for some inner meaning.

The reason we write poetry (and almost all of us do) is because we want to communicate: an ideal; an idea; or a specific feeling. Poetry is as essential in communication, as a letter; a radio; a telephone, and the main criterion for selecting the poems in this anthology is very simple: they communicate.

# CONTENTS

## When Peace Dawned Anew: 8th May '45

Memory lane is still leading us back
To those desperate years when days were so black;
When sirens were sounding and people were scared -
To their shelters they fled when war was declared.

Many cities were bombed, buildings fell to the ground.
Destruction was rife, stones and bricks all around.
Theatres and churches gone, little was spared
In those terrible raids after war was declared.

Brave men on the home front gave of their all
To bring food, drink and shelter and answer each call.
Seeing families made homeless with dearest ones dead
Was a sorrowful sight with streams of tears shed.

There seemed no ending - the war still raged free;
More killings at home and ships lost at sea.
Millions of Britons lost their lives in the fight,
Oh, never again must we face such a plight.

After five years of warfare, victory came fast.
The scourge of battle was over at last.
American GIs were VE day mad,
Throwing bottles and shouting - the scene was quite sad!

But as victory night passed and daylight broke through,
A new life began and peace dawned anew.
We will never forget the multitude who died -
They fought for their country and 'turned the tide'.

From battle to peace, that is how it must stay
Let's recapture the glory of that eighth day in May.

***Joyce Hemsley***

## A Sea Of Teardrops

Over seas of a million teardrops
On pastures of men's weary souls
Where fathers and sons stood united
Many dying not reaching their goals
Their blood was our rivers of freedom
Their pain our foundations to life
They stood strong to what lay before them
Stood proud in the hearts left behind
In defence of their own little island
They struggled through death sorrow and pain
Fallen comrades now immortal in marble
Stout cenotaphs bearing the strain
No medal too big for their glory
No ribbon too wide for their pain
So each let us all pay them homage
In the knowledge we'll meet them again.

***Brian Wardle***

## MISERIES OF WAR

The writer's pen flew across the page
Each word a work of art
And the story told unto the world
Came from the depths of his heart
The words told of infinite misery,
Of injustices and of strife,
Of man's incredible inhumanity
Total disregard for another's life.

Unbelievable for those whose lives
Untouched or tainted by persecution.
How could they have known, or even guessed
That the fate for most: was execution.
Even now the barbaric holocaust,
By some has been denied.
We are told 'it never happened'
Expected to believe, that no one died!

The writer himself a survivor.
Not so, the rest of his family and friends.
Engraved on his forearm . . . a number . . .
And in his heart; those inhuman events!
As he listens to the news on the wireless
Each and every other day
He relives his own personal agony
The images of torture and pain.

It seems to him, man will never learn
From the past mistakes of others,
For even today, men across the globe
Are killing their own brothers!
Perhaps the memories, when written down
May touch a cord in some
And stop in their tracks; their bigotry
Help prove the world can live as one!

***Gwyneth Wynn-Davies***

## I Will Remember

Though time and tide have washed your blood from beaches,
And no stone marks the ocean's deepest reaches.

Though tourists soar on freedom's bluest plain,
And no one weeps as fewer of the few remain.

Though shifting sands and deserts bury deep those mothers' sons,
And no bugle call can waken them nor rally rusted guns.

Though medals dull and ribbons fade and teardrops dry away,
I will my friends remember you, until my dying day.

***Eric J McClurry***

## THANK YOU

To all of you who fought and died on foreign fields,
Thank you.
To all of you who sought and tried to make a better world,
Thank you.
Your youth, your life, became the price,
A truly awesome sacrifice.
Yet still so many had to die
That I today may laugh and cry
And live my life quite free to do the things I choose,
It's thanks to you.
To those returned much older now, who took their country's call,
I, as youth, before you bow and thank you one and all.
For what you gave it's fair to say
Complacency abounds today.
So actors, pop stars, sportsmen too,
In humble admiration view
Those heroes of a greater sort,
Our liberty their actions bought.
But what value placed upon their offered souls,
By us, a blood red poppy,
By God, a key to all that heaven holds.

***Paula Maria McClurry***

## War Days

It was a year with much regret,
And one, that we should never forget,
Peace and quiet, a thing of the past,
When Hitler decided it wouldn't last,
Silvery moon, so lovely to see,
But knew it wasn't meant to be,
Air raids, shelters, bombs and guns,
Had many people on the run,
Soldiers, sailors, airmen too,
All had their jobs to do,
Sadness, hope and glory too
These were for the forgotten few,
Dunkirk seemed so far away,
But let's remember it was for you.

***Olive Moore***

## ANGELS' TEARS

I hear the angels weeping
As they watch the soldiers sleeping
The deepest final sleep they'll ever know.

Now they rest in heaven
Men from Cornwall and from Devon
The very best you'll ever know.

Cannon shells overhead are sighing
Above the screaming of the dying
Laying smashed and shattered down below.

Governments are barmy
Collecting taxes for the Army
And letting banks lend money to the foe.

I hear the angels crying
Bearing witness to the dying
Of youth so innocent
It had no personal foe.

***B D Vissian***

## JUMP TO GLORY

*(The following lines of verse are dedicated to the men of the Airborne Divisions who took part in the Arnhem Raid. It is an attempt to capture one of those timeless moments from which England's banner was woven.)*

A day in September, the year forty-four,
Rows of young men stood waiting to go,
Packed in the aircraft, quiet and calm
The sergeant's eyes shining, his upraised right arm.

Are you ready my lads, he said with a smile
It's not far to go, it will just take a while.
When I count to three out you will go,
No problem about it, straight down below.

Get rid of your chute and join your platoon,
I'll see that your dinner is ready at noon,
Then he was counting midst the noise and the flack,
Hurry up lads, come on young Jack.

Out through the door, then a rapid descent,
A jerk on the cords and then sailing they went,
Down through the sky, to face hell upon earth,
Remember the cost, and what it was worth.

***Jack Curtis***

## Individual Error

The night was dark, light rain it fell,
I lay there quick breathing, my turn and spell,
at clearing mines, a path and clearance.
An explosion overhead, a luminescent shell, its brilliance.
That bright white light showed all, exposed.

Then all hell let loose from machine gun chatter.
I clawed the soil, lie down low, who else would matter,
as I sank deep exposed to screaming tracer bullet.
Who knows that fear, all on your own, stomach in the gullet.
Deep screaming fear, lonely oblivion, militarily imposed.

I sank deep and as fast as anyone could,
the grassy hollow filled with rain, urine and mud,
as body, soil and rain ran incessant,
to fill the hollow below that screaming tracer crescent.
I clung to myself, praying and adrenaline well dosed.

The light faded down, to complete the blackness,
the tracers ceased, the chatter of death and terror madness.
I lay and lay till the dawn, a muddy mess, the earth's new-born.
I rolled to crouch and look about, a tattered minefield, forlorn.
Where is every man's pride, when stood amongst friends,
deathly reposed.

***Alan Noble***

## AIR RAID

The big, scary bombs
exploding up in the air.

The black, cloudy sky,
up there bombs flashing.

The German planes are not seen
by the searchlights.

The streets are empty;
no people there.

The sad, tired, people
are underground sleeping.

The war is here.

***Debbie Maxwell***

## AIR RAID

The evil enemies in their planes
dropping bombs everywhere.

Dark, silent, scary streets
is now empty

Scared, sad, strong, tired people
trying to get to sleep

This war now.

***Angela McCurdy***

## REMEMBERING

A once bright pair of twinkling eyes looks up towards the sky,
his mind flashing back to years gone by.
Who knows what thoughts stirred in that silvery grey head,
was he remembering friends, all now long dead?

Remembering the noise of planes, like thunder in the sky,
or trails of red and yellow flames leaping high.

Remembering in the pallid eerie light of dawn,
the sound of groaning engines - battered and torn,
limping home from battle,
weary and forlorn.

Remembering the screams, the fires, the carnage
and meanless destruction.

Remembering, the tears, the cries of the struggle
for that one last dying breath,
as both young and old fight desperately to escape,
the angel of death.

Remembering those brave young friends with hearts so strong and true,
remembering how they fought for life,
remembering how he was one of the lucky few.

Remembering with the passing of time, broken hearts and homes
will mend,
but the vivid images of war, stay with you until the end.

***Susan Revell***

## Let Us Remember Them

Record their names as we recall
The reason why they gave their all.
In khaki brown, two shades of blue
They gave their all for me and you.
Those boys and girls of yesteryear
Are still in memory ever dear.
Their names are on no page or stone
Who will remember? When we are gone!
Let us record them, while we can
Who sacrificed their all for man;
Just stop: just think, and say a prayer,
To show that we still really care
And that our prayers will never cease
To find for the world everlasting peace.

***Mary Watson***

## THE YOUNG SOLDIER

With frightened eyes he looked around,
At comrades - dead upon the ground.
From eager throats had come the cry,
'Kill or be killed - conquer or die!'

They'd marched out like men, with a target in view,
The right of their cause had carried them through.
They'd all fought like fiends, through those hours of hell,
Through blasting of bomb, - and whining of shell.

Like a man he had fought - with courage and joy,
But stood now a terrified shivering boy.
The air filled with silence, the fighting was done,
Though his comrades he'd lost, the battle was won.

The groans of the dying, the smell of the dead,
Brought tears to his eyes and a heart full of dread.
And his stomach heaved at this terrible sight,
For he *was* just a boy, and too young to fight.

Gone was the glory, his heart filled with pain,
As he wept for the friends that he'd not see again.
With a mind growing old, this youngster now saw,
The sadness, stupidity, cruelty of war.

***Dorothie E Stalton***

## EARTH END . . .

We live
on a dying planet
where the atmosphere -
the seas, the rivers
and the once fertile soil
are poisoned by toxic waste.

Acid rain falls to earth
destroying woodlands
and the greenlife of our sphere . . .
this foul water is engendered
by big fat cat profits
for the favoured few

Ruthless cruelty spreads
across the blood-stained world
people exterminate their neighbours
as men, women, children
and even tiny babies
are slaughtered without mercy.

War is the ultimate obscenity
and its evil virus
contaminates our planet Earth
as violence dominates our lives
while compassion and pity
are destroyed for evermore.

Why do we behave
in such mindless barbaric ways
when we are all human beings
existing on this tiny globe
within a vast universe
beyond our feeble understanding?

***Stephen Gyles***

## EVACUEES (1941-1945)

*(Dedicated to Robert Spruce and family)*

Being evacuated when you are eight years old,
Is not hard to comprehend,
Just re-think the memories
From beginning to end.

Two young lads from Liverpool,
Heading out of town,
Gas masks and a bar of chocolate,
But not knowing where you're bound.

We ended up in 'Highley',
A village near - 'Bridgnorth',
To escape the German bombers,
And the atrocities of war.

Not knowing our fate or destiny,
We had to stand our ground,
And waited until selected,
By a local female hand.

Her name was Mrs Walker,
She said you call me Nan,
But this lady was no substitute,
For the person we called 'Mam'.

Life was a game of survival,
Competing with the rest,
The local village children,
The countryside and all its pests.

We didn't have many comforts,
Or solace when in pain,
Especially when potato picking,
In the pouring rain.

We survived the mumps and whooping cough,
And goose grease on your chest,
But scabies between your fingers,
That really was the test.

A boil on your bum was something else,
That no one could explain,
And then a 'kaolin poultice',
Just to relieve the pain.

When the war was ended in 1945,
I can look back in retrospect now I'm sixty-five,
We have lots of happy memories, my kid brother and me
It wasn't all bad, being an evacuee!

***H Croston***

## Island Fortress

The war against evil was fought and won
A battle of iron wills bruising and long
The price paid in blood of each nation's sons
Fought with malicious intent with bravery and guns
Families waiting at home in dread and in fear
Bombers heard overhead on destruction hell bent
These purveyors of death by Hitler were sent
So few against so many in the battle for skies above
Hurricane and Spitfire fight together like hand in glove
The larger enemy defeated driven back from our shores
The RAF beat the odds and evened the scores
Our island fortress a haven for those who are oppressed
Was battered and scarred but stood up to he test
The Royal Navy fought battles on the world's oceans and seas
They chased the Nazi Naval machine and brought it to its knees
These islands are small but the will of the people is not
They had to be strong to beat Hitler's Nazi plot

***James Carlin Hughes***

## A Candle In The Window

A candle in the window
Its flame is burning bright
Carrying a spark of hope
With its flickering light

For in the east there is a war
That threatens all mankind
Armies from around the world
Unite to fight a common foe
To save us from a holocaust
We need this candle's glow

Its spark will generate
Unison for good it will create
As long as it shall burn
Our world will never mourn
The loss of all mankind

So place a candle in your window
Keep hope burning bright
A candle in your window
Will help us win this fight.

***Jim Nicol***

## Come And Gone

The Germans are coming
So are the bombs
Children are screaming
Separated from their mums

Into the shelter
Safe and sound
Here comes a bomb spinning round like a helter-skelter
The howling stopped as it thundered to the ground

Another bomb is coming
With the last person running
Oh, he just made it
As the planes started humming

Two hours have passed
The Germans have left at last
People searching for their houses
Like little lost mouses

Voices screaming like hurricanes
People crying with burst veins
Buildings crashing
And torches flashing

I smell fumes
Like a thousand perfumes
Makes me sick
In the middle of a tip
Which is actually . . . *The Blitz*

***Stuart Faskin (11) Aberdeenshire***

## UNTITLED

When I was young, oh eight or nine
The whole world was at war
And widows wept while loved ones 'slept'
Out on a foreign shore
Mothers said 'Goodbye' to sons
Barely in their teens
For some of them, their life was done
A few more broken dreams
A promise of blood toil and tears was made
But never mind
They also promised us the earth
When this was all behind
Win the war, there'll be no more
Grief and poverty
A home for everybody, medication free
There would be full employment
A nation filled with pride
We'd be the envy of the world
For this our brave had died
But somehow things did not work out
The way they should have done
All the promises they made
Were broken one by one
The dole queue is now higher
Than any time before
Was somebody a liar
When they said we'd won the war?

***Joan Dalkin***

## FREEDOM'S PRICE

Shoulder to shoulder, oh, how proud they were that day!
Long lines, short lines, of blue and brown and grey
Eyes right, colours bright, glistening in the morning sun
Hearts trembled, all assembled, for the job that had to be done.

Rolling seas, shaking knees, as they plunged on into the spray
Live young! Die young! were the shouts they heard that day
Loud screams, fearful dreams, were the sounds that filled the night
Was he married? Yeah, he was married. Oh, what a terrible sight.

But still they came, the halt and lame, on into the battle's fray
Long lines, short lines, of blue and brown and grey
A wagging finger, no time to linger, or even say a prayer
For friends lost, don't count the cost, just leave them lying there.

And now they rest, the very best, who gave all they had to give
God cried as each one died, before they even had a chance to live
Hearts stilled, dreams unfulfilled, cut down like a sheaf of corn
Yet hope springs, on passion's wings, for a new and brighter dawn.

Long lines, short lines, beneath the sky they lay
Shoulder to shoulder, oh, how proud they were that day
No more fears, no more tears, as onward to Heaven they go
For this was the price to be paid for the peace that we who are left
shall know.

***Jean Tabley***

## VE Day

How time has flown since VE Day
Our toddlers are truly married
We'd blacked out room - poor rations but -
Our determination never flurried

We worked our fingers - to the bone
To keep - the Union Jack - flying
Obeyed the rules - shared our food
And watched out for Germans spying

Then once the war was truly won
It was time to start - to thrive
But first - we must thank our God
That we were all - still alive

We took down all the blackouts - quick
And - all the churchbells - they were rung
A children's party - organised
And - all gave goodies - and people sung

The lamps were lit at teatime
Towns again - had their name plates
One could buy some new clothing
And fires - burnt in our grates

Folks all cheered on VE Day
For - yes - the victory had been won
But - yet - many a family had been saddened
By the loss of a father - or a son.

***Edna A M Cattermole***

## AIR RAID

The scary, frightening bombs
        Roaring through the air

The big German planes
        Bombing everywhere

The tired, dirty, old and young
        Cheering themselves underground

The dark, silent streets
        Waiting patiently for an end

The bright, big searchlights
        Sweeping the sky for Germans

The dark, smoky sky
        Lit up like a firework display

Be alert for the siren

***Stuart McKay***

## THE AIR RAID

The bright, exploding bombs
whistling through the air

Black, smoky, fiery sky
bright with flashing lights

Empty, dirty streets
charred by smoke-filled incendiaries

The huge, enemy German planes
droning yet unsighted

Sad but singing people
tired, cold and hiding

The air raid starts once more.

***Suzanne McCall***

## AIR RAID

The frightened, scary whistling bombs
wailing in the sky

The empty, dusty, smoke-filled streets
Where the bombed down houses lie

The huge, German enemy planes
looking for the warships

The black, crowded moonlight sky
full of planes and smoke

The scared, tired, grubby people
cold and full of fear

This is what it's like
when Hitler's rage is here.

***Kieran Donald***

## Air Raid

The loud, scary bombs
Exploding in the night.

The dark, shadowy sky
Crowded by the planes.

The silent, empty streets
Bombed every day.

The huge, German planes
Fly over Britain each night.

The scared, tired people
Cold but still alive.

***Sharlene Spencer***

## AN AIR RAID

The dark, black, inky sky
lit up by flashing lights.

The broken down streets
charred and abandoned.

Cold, grubby, people
singing underground.

German and British planes
drowning us in noise.

The dreadful, loud, bombs
whistling and wailing.

***John McIntosh***

# Raid

Dreadful, scary bombs
falling from above
Inky, black sky
lighted by fiery bombs
Silent, deserted streets
crowded by charred buildings
Droning, enemy planes
dropping bombs on us
Sad, cold people
hiding from the bombs
Bright, silent search lights
looking for German planes.

*The war has begun.*

***David Kelly***

## AIR RAID

The sounds of the bombs
silently dropping

The black cloudy sky
filled with smoke and dust

Streets are covered in rubble
as disaster strikes the ground

German planes fly over London
faster than a bullet

People scared and frightened
as noise is drowned out.

This is war.

***Darren McLoughlin***

## AIR RAID

The scary, whistling bombs
  flying through the night sky.

The Germans up there
  dropping bombs down here.

The people, scared and tired;
  when will they get sleep?

The black, inky sky
  with the enemy about to die.

The silent, empty streets
  with lots of dust and smoke.

Now hear the all clear.

***Kevin Speirs***

## War Raid

The empty and deserted streets
abandoned but filled with smoke.

The dark sky is now crowded
and the noise is getting louder.

The huge German planes are here
they were unsighted by the British.

The dreadful bombs so silent
but then they glow with a whine.

The surviving people are scared but strong
in their cheerful singing.

The search lights looking for planes
they won't give up, they'll find them.

The air raid has now begun.

***Daniel Watson***

## Air Raid

The frightening, wailing bombs
sailing through the air

The cheery, thoughtful people
sharing what they've got

The huge, noisy planes
hiding in the clouds

The empty, rubbled streets
dusty from the bombs

The black, inky sky
lit up by the moonlight

The war is here!

***Karen Ogilvie***

## They Gave Their Tomorrows

Young men of every race and creed,
Flocked to the colours during Britain's greatest need.
With selfless thought and no little pride,
They stood against the Nazi tide.

From the early darkest days of war,
No one doubted what they struggled for.
On a small French beach, Dunkirk was its name,
They won themselves everlasting fame.
Then standing firm on our own good soil,
The Nazi fury hit its boil.

On they came like darkened clouds,
Death and destruction raining down.
But all through that terrible blitz,
The British spirit gave not one bit.
Into the clouds our young boys soared,
And decimated the German hoard.

Life in the convoys was hard and tough,
The U-boat packs closed in at dusk.
Many a good ship never reached its port,
Sad reading filled the report.

Then on a bright summer's morning on a Normandy beach,
German might at last was breached.
In different battles in far flung lands,
Their blood stained the earth and sand.
Victory won at no small cost, freedom takes a terrible loss.

All these years later, let us not forget,
We owe these people an unpayable debt.
For the freedom we take as our God given right,
They raged against the dying of the light.

***Robert Scally***

## Memories

Gods of war never to be satisfied
So many virtuous people have died
What makes it that you are always so cruel
Heartbreak sadness to you are usual.

Harry Woods that impish lad at his school
Always smiling sometimes playing the fool
Said goodbye to mother and then a wave
Now lies in a watery, unknown grave.

Jack Bond that lad good at every sport
Helping everyone just as he ought
Was a crew member of an aeroplane
Plunged into the sea, not heard of again.

People innocently doing shopping
Carefully looking at their rationing
Suddenly the sound of a flying bomb
Cutting out it became their tomb.

Bill Dods the student everyone knew
Changed from the Medical Corps to tank crew
Cut to pieces from a tank piercing round
No mothers mourning, remains never found.

When at last War Gods you have had your fill
You cared not for your work for good or ill
Hibernation you took from evil work
Mankind from its duty will not shirk.

***Peter A Butcher***

## The War To End All Wars

Trenches, deep and filled with rain,
The atmosphere charged with fear and pain,
Mud, thick, cold, cloying, ankle deep,
Men ceased to care; they longed for sleep.

Over the top, brave men falling,
Officers urging, crying, shouting, calling,
Onward, forward, 'Let us go to our death,
Will we be remembered as we take our last breath?'

Guns booming, shells exploding,
Stench of death and bodies folding,
Barbed wire clutching at men's hands,
Cavernous holes looming in no-man's-land.

Think of these gory scenes from Hell,
No pictures, films or words can ever tell,
The horror of this daily scene,
As the battle rages and bullets scream.

Countless men died; they gained a few yards,
Life was always but a game of cards,
The flower of youth was cruelly cut down,
The earth was covered by a blood-red gown.

The sun was obscured by clouds of gas and polluted air,
Darkness of soul and spirit was always there,
Yet they never faltered, suffered and bled,
Horses and men, limbs severed, cried until they were dead.

Remember always this was done in our name,
They never searched for glory or fame,
Pass the proud Cenotaph and whisper low,
'May the memory of your brave deeds forever glow.'

***Irene Greenall***

## THE UNITED NATIONS

The Bird of Death swoops low and grand,
Plucking lives from the raging land
Of guns and bombs, where dismay is planned,
And mourning of the dead,
Is war the only way?

The Bird of Death picks anyone,
German, American, all are one,
It only lives when wars rage on,
Where legions of people die,
Is war the only way?

The Bird of Death has feathers red,
Distinct black bands round feet and head.
Red, the blood of soldiers dead,
The black bands of despair,
Is war the only way?

From the embers of war begins a glow,
In veins where anger and pain did flow,
Understanding and hope begin to grow.
A seed is sown in the heart of man,
Is war the only way?

So as we charge to the Y2K,
Let the Phoenix emerge from the disarray,
Rising up as we throw our weapons away,
And listen when I tell you this,
War is *not* the way.

***Rickie L Jackson***

## Now We Know

We did not know,
nor know the people who were in the know.
But after Poland, Britain went to fight
against injustice and the Nazi might.

We did not know
about the racism and persecutions, so
just like their dads - on them we would depend
to halt the tyranny; free will defend.

We did not know
that war had changed and Dunkirk was a blow
that nearly finished freedom for our land.
But rather than submit we made a stand.

We did not know
air raids. Civilian deaths would bring us low.
Pearl Harbour and the Yanks came to our aid.
The Second front and the price that we all paid.

We did not know
the horrors concentration camps would show.
The millions of homeless on the move.
Communist views that we could not approve.

We did not know
the shock atomic warfare soon would sow
across the world; years of distrust and hate.
Mankind was asking now - is it too late?

We did not know
or realise that they gave up their life
that we could live in freedom, without strife.
To all the dead our gratitude we show.
For *now* we know.

***Ida Shewan***

## THE POPPIES

Every time a plane flies overhead, I still tense -
Afraid of what it once meant.
Lying down in the shelter, hour after hour,
Whilst the fear was immense.

Iron railings still make me remember the War,
Changed into munitions in the factories roar!
Ever resourceful, 'Make-do-and-mend',
Spirits lifted, normal life at an end.

An old wireless sends my memory back.
Trying to hear the news, trying to keep track -
What's happening in France? Has Hitler retreated?
Praying for time when he would be defeated.

But those poppies, which dance on a summer's day,
Always remind me where our loved ones lay.
Their petals, so intense and splashed with fire
Bring the most precious memories - those which never tire.

***S Wood***

## YEARS NOT MORROWS

There'd been wars before, since time began,
Where men had marched to glory,
But this war's different they all said,
And not the same old story.

Mothers cried and sent their sons
With anguished hearts and sorrow,
Some waved goodbye with zeal and pride
T'will be over by the morrow.

'The war to end all wars,' the papers cried,.
So send your sons and thousands died,
In fields of gore for years, not morrows,
In foreign country sides.

Mothers waited through the years,
With dread in hearts and hidden tears,
With 'Missing in Action' heard still in their ears,

While the men were gone the children grew,
Into young men - don't take them too.
For years not morrows, the men did strive
To keep us free to stay alive.

Up to their necks in blood and stenches,
Homesick for both hearth and home,
And loved ones left behind alone
With only photographs and memories
Of why they were in this gory place,
To fight for freedom and solace.

That peace may come again once more,
And take them home from foreign shore
That life be back as was before,
Of this we should remember, lest not forget
The men who fought for years not morrows,
And earned mankind's respect.

***Maureen Moore***

## How High The Price?

I really will not forget you, you are like a picture all faded and worn,
You died for me and my country just as I was born.

I watch the war on the movie screen and shudder at the sight,
But I forget how high the price was as I get on with my life.
The films are worn and tattered and are now becoming a grind;
Yet my family have never forgotten, you are firmly fixed in our mind.

I look at your faded old photo' and the dog tags I hold in my hand,
Without you my gallant hero, there would be no freedom in this land.

God opened the gateway to heaven and took you into His fold,
As you gave your life for your country, with no chance
to ever grow old.

***Barbara Tyers***

## VE Day - Memories Of A Banner

I fluttered above the village green
and danced with revellers below.
My banner friends in ample abundance,
fought for space, their colours dazzling
in the June sunlight.

Children, bellies full of 'gobstoppers' romped
among buttercups like buzzing bluebottles,
while parents gossiped in a sea of
communal joy.

Trestle tables bulged with 'Spam' sandwiches
and sugar-free 'goodies'.
Home brewed beer, headless, fast disappearing,
sought shelter from the heat of the day.

'Tipperary' tunes monopolised the day
as dancers kicked high - showing 'utility knickers'.
Khaki clad soldiers, peacock proud in victory
hugged their giggling sweethearts.
Happiness was everywhere.

***Alex Branthwaite***

## THE LANCASTER

Immobile, it lies shrouded in its hangar,
Black and forbidding, without a scratch.
Two brothers preserved it in memory of Cris.
The body is perfect, shows no patch.

A museum behind is full of memories
Pictures and keepsakes when the Lancaster flew.
A background of music from the '40s haunts
The listeners who remember air crew.

Appeals hang on the wall for information
Of fathers and uncles long since dead.
Did they die in vain that no one remembers?
'Probably shot down' is casually said.

Now turned to ashes or dust, relations still hunger
For someone who knew them; a clue to their death.
Maybe a witness was there when they crashed,
Held them as they breathed their last breath.

The dead are remembered by siblings and children.
We who lost nobody think of them too.
Fifty years after the Second World War
Their sacrifice valued all the world through.

Inside the black body the engines roar
To no purpose; maybe one day she'll be
Aloft in the air. . . but meanwhile
The ghost of the Lancaster flies in the memory.

***Jane England***

## Forget Not Freedom's Vanguard

Consumerism loosed our world,
Nations fought markets for trade;
Eat, drink and be merry unfurled,
The starving never made the grade.
The nineteen thirties were dark times,
Spanish civil war sparked crimes.

Never forget Nazi Hitler,
Allied with Mussolini;
Millions massacred with whittler,
Hate raged with ignominy,
Mad psychopathic maniacs.
Jews gassed by demoniacs.

The holocaust of Europe's Jews,
Changed the wide world's consciousness.
Auschwitz slave camp run by yahoos,
Grim horror no righteousness.
Daily they faced cold, hunger, grief;
Suffering with no relief.

We praise the great, venturesome, strong;
Thousands gave all and perished.
Staunch of strength they conquered the wrong,
Their chivalry is cherished.
We pledge service that pays the price,
Undiminished sacrifice.

Men nailed the Lord on wood, His throne;
He claimed 'I am the world's light'
Matchless His love for worthless shown,
Brings freedom with Spirit's might.
Giver of justice, supreme good;
Makes our world one neighbourhood.

***James Leonard Clough***

## Elegy To The Fallen War Dead

A war to end all wars.
The greatest war of them all,
Succeeded by yet one more.
Though the second was born of necessity,
Not of folly.
For in the heartland of Europe there had been born a ravenous tyranny,
That fell without remorse;
A bullet in the brain.

To the East a sun did set,
On a land of pride and wisdom that learned its lesson,
Along with the rest in our bloody digression;
To the holocaust of a nuclear dawn;
Wreaked by the country that for five cold decades held its finger upon
the trigger;
Locked in the stalemate of power-struggle with the motherland that
scorched her earth.

For six raging years the darker demons of our nature ran amuck,
Rampant in the wake of our bloody muck;
Laughed with glee at the rubble of the Blitz,
The firestorm,
And poison black rain.
They lay with the many in the mass graves;
All the more happy for the gross genocide.
They marched with the soon to be dead;
All the more happy when they fell by the wayside.
Took to the seas and skies;
Dragged down with joy men, women and boys.

Still they lie with the dead at rest;
Those fallen millions who all at once utter the solemn cathartic whisper,
So that they might not come amongst us again;
Lest we forget.
Lest we forget.
Lest we forget.

***Matthew C Plumb***

## FORGOTTEN MOTHERS

And I cuddled the child
That made the man.
I gave you the soldier
You sent to a war
That is no more.

But where is the man
That grew from a boy,
That marched in time
With all the others,
Who kissed their sweethearts
And hugged their mothers?

I will tell you where.
He's over there,
Name etched in stone
With a marble border,
Alphabetically placed in order.

Gone is the conflict,
Mortars and guns.
Yet we are still mothers
And those were our sons.

***Doreen Nicolson***

## TORQUAY, SUNDAY MAY 29TH 1943

*(From a penthouse overlooking the bay)*

As on the floor I lie,
I can see the enemy in the sky.
Terror and gunfire all around,
Remembering my brother's words 'Get on the ground.'
His wise advice was really sound,
It saved our lives as our hearts did pound.

The bomb finally did fall,
Leaving us beneath a blackened pall.
An eerie silence then descended,
We prayed that it at last had ended.
Fear returned - was there a fire?
Was this to be our funeral pyre?

The roof above was blown away,
Allowing the sun to make its way.
Unfortunately this lovely sight,
Was not the end of our chronic plight.
The main approach was no longer there,
So we had to find another stair.
Through the debris and the gloom,
We made our way from room to room.

Now out a window, down the rungs,
The air was bursting in our lungs.
One more home down below,
To complete the way we had to go.
Safely on the road that day,
We saw a sight that caused dismay.
Devastation all around,
Those we knew lay on the ground.

With heavy hearts we walked away,
And 57 years on, I still pray.
'Stop the nonsense that we recall,
And make the world safe for us all.'

***Peter Foreman***

## COCK CROW

War service with the Gurkhas in Burma long ago
Meant marching many miles each day on little jungle tracks.
The bulky loads went on the mules, but we had heavy packs
And on the ground at night we slept till dawn began to show.
Most mornings at the dawn Stand-to a distant cock would crow
And now when, after fifty years, I hear that sound again
My mind goes back to Burma and our cheerful little men
Preparing for what lay ahead, which none of us could know.

***Ian Purvis***

## SEPTEMBER 1939

Now are the mighty fallen,
The strength of man has gone;
Nought can be accomplished,
When love and truth pass on.

Now are the mighty fallen,
The tide doth backward flow,
Brotherhood lies vanquished
And joy gives place to woe.

How are the mighty fallen
And hate and fear enthroned?
Can we e'er restore them
These monarchs that we stoned?

Love will not bow to envy
Nor claims of selfish creeds;
Cries of men are empty
When they are damned by deeds.

***Norman Dudley***

## Is The War Over?

Down in this trench, I'm in the front line,
Waiting and thinking to pass the time.
I look up at the sky, by now it's black,
I'm waiting for the enemy to attack.

Loud thundery noise, the sky flashes white,
Was it a bomb or a grenade which made the light?
I'm so scared, I want to move back,
There goes the order, it's time to attack.

I move without thinking, I get up and go,
Shooting my gun, did I hit? I don't know.
I jump to the floor with mud in my face,
I ran so fast, I would have won if it was a race.

The enemy moves back, it must be a retreat,
The sound of surrender sounds so sweet.
It's time to clear up, it's time to go
Is the war over, does anyone know?

***J Cross***

## A Battle For Britain

Smoke trails black in a clear summer sky,
Spitfire, Hurricane circling high,
German formations break and run,
as planes swoop down coming in from the sun.

Rat tat tat tat the machine guns burst,
as pilots and gunners expect the worse.
Airfields and cities the targets are clear,
to break the will and instil fear.

We are the target of Hitler's might,
but they are the few who will carry the fight,
over channel, cornfield, city and town,
keeping us safe from the blood-snarling hound.

In these dark days, as we stand alone,
bravely defending our island home,
while Europe's engulfed by a blackening foam
of swastika banner and guttural tone.

If we can survive then others may see,
the shining light of liberty,
and know that they may yet be free.

***Michelle Fermer***

## BENGHAZI

*(For my good friend Harry McDonald, who fought alongside thousands of his comrades in the desert with the 8th army in the Second World War)*

I'm sick of the sand and the constant drone
Of the flies in this arid place,
The squaddies who always gripe and moan
And let down the Corps in disgrace.

I'm proud to be one of the 'Desert Rats'
Though I curse all this sand at will,
And envy the lot of the top 'Brass-hats'
With their comfort and shade from the hill.

But I'm not one of the moaning brigade
A hardened old sweat of the line,
Rommel may come, still I'm seldom afraid,
With my Lee-Enfield rifle I'm fine.

Sand in our tea, sand in our stew,
And sand in all that we eat;
In careless lads' boots a scorpion or two,
Our bodies demented with prickly heat.

We covet the shade, read mail from home,
And hide from the searing sky,
That strips the very flesh from your dome,
And burns out the sight from your eye.

It's March now; thoughts fly home to Spring,
And cool long walks by the Trent.
A welcoming pint a landlord would bring,
This is living, and how it was meant.

You long for wind and rain and frost,
With chattering teeth fighting cold,
And pray you're not one paying the cost,
But with luck, to return to grow old.

***John MacLean***

## The Oosterbeek Perimeter - Arnhem September 1944

Look out beyond the bounds
   from where the rows of headstones stand,
to where in 1944
   the air was full of jagged splinter,
searing shot,
   and men did scream.
And die.

Then go beyond those bounds
   and touch the ground that felt
the splash of blood and crash of shell.
   And touch the new grown shoots
that have their roots,
   in tortured Hell.

Then, from beyond the bounds
   turn back and see this place
with different eye.
   And cry.

***Peter Gibson***

## Ode To 617 Squadron

With quiet determination Barnes Wallis carefully planned
An unbelievable strategy to save our great England.
Perhaps, when he was only young, he threw stones upon the sea:
So he designed a bouncing bomb to cause floods in Germany.

His plan of action ready, he knew what he had to do -
He went off to St Vincent's to meet Guy Gibson and his crew.
It was to squadron 617 that the heavy burden fell:
Destroy the walls of the German Dams, then return home, safe and well.

The action was top secret and at the dead of night,
The bomber crews checked height and speed to be exactly right.
The barrel-shaped bombs dropped silently and bounced
towards the dams
As airmen watched with bated breath, floods engulfed the hostile land.

So many men did not return to their families back home.
They gave the final sacrifice, their fate was left unknown.
Now, even after fifty years, we salute the squadron's name
And their mission is forever told in Petwood's Hall of Fame.

***Judith Anne Percival***

## Wartime Remembered

I was born in nineteen thirteen
And I remember four of them.
In the first one no ration books
So it passed from mouth to mouth
As fast as one could utter
That one shop had some butter.
Folk turned up full of hope
To join the queue
But never knew
Until the *sold out* call was made
Then the queue would gradually fade
And hope for better luck another day.

Once my mother changed her hat and went again,
The duty policeman gave my mother just a wink
And let her through
For well he knew
There were two families to feed
So let her pass.

***Phyllis Dunn***

## TEARS ON A POPPY

A soldier in a shell-hole lies
Pain and sadness dull his eyes
And time his young life ebbs away
On shattered chalk and clinging clay
Mud caked the uniform he wears
Khaki, blue or drab field grey
It matters not for on this day
All are martyrs to the fray.

Machine guns chatter their angry fire,
Lead hornets pinging off the wire
An orchestra of great guns thunder
The trembling earth is rent asunder
And shrapnel thick as winter hail
Falls, the blasted ground to flail
Whilst tendrils of miasmic gas
Taint the mutilated grass.

Peace restored to this tortured field
Its fertile soil once more to yield
A growing golden stand of grain
Washed by drops of silver rain
Which adorn the scarlet poppies' bloom
Where mother earth doth e'er entomb
Tears for men from this life torn,
Tears for their children - never born.

***Robert E Fraser***

## Memories Of War

During the years of queuing for food and rationing,
Of coupons for clothes and blackout curtaining;
My husband was called up to go over there,
He went, into the army, I knew not where.
For weeks and months; no news.
Then we heard of Dunkirk, the people there, refugees,
Fleeing from homes, prams loaded with food and babies,
And our armies were retreating to the shore.
Then our ships and boats went across the channel,
To try and save men's lives.
The enemy bombed the rescue ships great and small,
Those on the top decks were wounded by shrapnel,
Some were helped to better shelter down below
Suffering from wounds; many lives were saved; to go Deal or Dover.
At last a letter came on one fine summer's day.
Bad news, but it told us where the wounded lay:
I remember gardens, all the flowers in bloom,
And long bus journeys.
Then out of hospital for some compassionate leave:
Before training for the desert war; no time to grieve.
I went to help my dad and brothers, because Mum was ill:
I remember the Blitz, and the sound of sirens still,
And our good neighbours.
When I wrote to tell the news, a baby's on the way
One brother thought it wrong in wartime:
My husband wrote to say
Please go and live with my people
That would be better
Dear little girl, he'd started the letter,
How silly, I thought, being twenty-four.

***E Apps***

## POPPIES

The poppies are swaying in the cold breeze
They seem to bow their heads,
And pray with their leaves.
Moving backwards and forwards in waves,
Like a large red blanket
To cover the young men's graves.
For there's a red poppy growing,
For each man that has died
And they are all watered
By every tear that is cried.
The poppies grow on, forever,
For years and years to come.
For each lonely widow,
For every mother and father who mourns a son.
The poppies stand tall now,
Not like so many young men.
Cut down in their prime, never to breathe again,
So there's no sound of marching now.
No military parades
No roll call of honours
No bugle to be played.
There's just an eerie silence,
That and the scent of poppies will not fade.
For forever a blanket will cover the brave.

***Trudie Sullivan***

## Pilots A Few

It was my childhood desire to fly a spitfire.
To be the victor so brave against the odds.
A time of warriors to admire, a time of justifiable carnage being a flyer.
To kill or be killed, to hunt the Hun in the sun.
A glorified war, one of many crusades to acquire peace and freedom,
Stability to admire.
At what cost bravery a medal to require.

***Barrie S Allport***

## My War

Looking back, as I recall,
My war was not too bad at all:
Volunteered at just nineteen,
First time from home that I had been,
Born and bred to country ways
I little knew how wartime days
Would change my life - those pastures new
In uniform of Air Force blue.
First Padgate to receive my kit
Then square bashing to make me fit:
Once AI then off to learn,
No time for homeward thoughts to turn,
Nine months later, trade in hand,
Skilled wireless Mech - coastal command,
A few months' stint then posted to
Service 'fighters' - help 'the few',
Then to the main job of my war -
Lancasters in Lincolnshire
'Twas there I met a special friend,
Like brothers we, till war did end:
By which time I had a wife,
Looked forward to a brand new life.
Five years flew past so very fast
Till victory was won at last.
Where now are all those mates I met,
Faces that I won't forget:
Some names though lost in mists of time,
My war in thirty lines of rhyme,
Five years, though not spectacular -
My contribution to the war.

***Peter Fordham***

## THE SACRIFICE

In rows we stood,
So proud and tall,
To serve our country,
One and all.

In rows we stood,
Our intentions clear,
To give freedom to,
The ones so dear.

In rows we marched,
Our futures bleak,
Aware of the dangers,
From the enemies we seek.

In rows we marched,
Stories growing more,
Trying to forget about,
What the future had in store.

In rows we fell,
How afraid we were,
Men of all ages,
Falling near and far.

In rows we fell,
The fear of feeling cold,
Men of all backgrounds,
Their stories never to be told.

***Lisa Jane Hall***

## WHAT'S THE REASON FOR

In a poppy field - is where Tommy lies
tears have all long since cried
when Tommy got the call - be proud lad
take the King's shilling - said his dad
it'll be over by Christmas, they all said
to a foreign shore - they marched away
some never seeing another English day
but Christmas came and Christmas went
but Tommy never knew.
Little did they know - Tommy would be dead
blindfolded - when the bullets flew
Still echoing in his ears - be proud lad - be proud
a poppy petal - is every Tommy's heart
every beat - a dream - a hope
soon war was no more - escaping back by boat
Tommy's trunk - was locked away
never again to see the light of day
Tommy marched away to play his part
a locked trunk of memories - never mends a broken heart
be proud lad - be proud - is the ghostly echo
what the poppy has come to symbolise.

***David Charles***

## Remembering

Fifty-five years ago there ended a war
we vowed then there would be no more
in nineteen eighteen they said the same
but in nineteen thirty-nine it started again

Brave men were called up to learn to fight
but when they were trained ho what a sight
they came from all walks of life
and went off to war behind drum and fife

They fought a brave war in the air and sea
on land they were at Alemain, Tobruck and Tripoli
as well as Italy they went ashore at Normandy
and they didn't stop till they got into Germany

Let's not forget those in the Far East heat
in the swamps and the jungles they did compete
in the end the enemy were in retreat
with two atomic bombs they admitted defeat

With the war over we did congratulate
with VE and VJ street parties we had to celebrate
we vowed then there would be no more
fifty-five years ago when we ended that war

***M Birks***

## 50 Years On

We're celebrating VE day plus
Fifty years on, why all the fuss?
To tell the young a story true
Of gallant lads, who fought for you.

Mock not at the old and weak
They once were proud and at their peak
Who fought for King and country well
Some didn't make it, many fell.

From Dunkirk to El Alamein
Across to Burma and back again
By the wayside, many died
Comrades felt guilty that *they* survived!

Those that live, are fighting still
For a decent pension, the right to be ill
A hospital bed should be their due
Remember, that they fought for you!

Honour the photo on the wall
Of Gran's husband, young and tall
Honour the medals, tossed in a drawer
He got them for helping to win the war.

Remember them all, as you celebrate
And let no one forget this date
Pray those lives weren't lost in vain
That such a war won't come again

For, without those young men
Brave and true,
Just think of this -
There'd be no you!

***A Burman***

## DUNKERQUES HEROES

Dunkerque, Dunkerque a special place
It has so many memories
Of blood shed on its beaches
Of soldiers stranded on the dunes
Fearing for their lives
They couldn't sleep, there wasn't time

Big ships and little boats
To their rescue came
As they waded in the water
They were bombed from overhead
Many drowned who could not swim
Hands stretched out to help them
Pulling tired soldiers on their decks

They were saddened by their comrades falling
But were glad to be alive
Many risked their lives to save
Bonds were formed, new friendships made

God was watching over one and all
He saw his people home
Plucked from the jaws of death
A victory had been won
They will always be remembered
Those brave and gallant men
God let your love shine through
So no more wars will be
But peace will reign instead.

***Pamela D Jewell***

## THE WASTED YEARS

*(To my friend Edward, rear gunner in Lancaster's Royal Air Force Tangmere and Winthorpe 1942/43)*

Not for me to fire the gun; 'to blast to hell the bloody hun'
But for me the humble chore - to keep the cameras clean and
focused right -
So that this young and sensitive chap, confined, confused, in turret trap
May stand a fifty-fifty chance, by fighting mist, cloud and streaking rain
Of landing safe and coming home again.

And at 'take off', as terror sickens, and in agony
Green spews o'er the turret floor, as death rides with this young chap
With pale pinched face, with throbbing heart - contracting loin
Wonders why on earth he'd ever joined!

I cannot give my life for him who should have so many years to come
Living, high living - for Liz, and Mum.
To me - with many years behind,
Life is not so much
In contemplation of death's inevitable clutch.

What is this? - A crippled craft?
Perforated tank, a fractured prop, the lot!
And things now to face,
Vomit, blood and guts about the place
And a young moaning thing
A treasured thing, at least for one,
A son, now crying out in agony - for Mum.

Oft' have I had to strike away the hot and welling tears
In contemplation of Those Wasted Years

***S H Vick***

## Salute The Soldier

They loved their Scottish homeland
and scented English lanes,
They loved the great Welsh mountains
and the soft summer rains,
But now they sleep in Burma
where the river Chindwin flows.
A small white cross above their heads
their names their comrades know.

They loved their little village streets
where lights did gleam like pearls,
They loved the pictures, and to dance
with pretty village girls,
Their youth was a brief glory
which sped too swiftly by,
They left their happy homeland
and crossed the sea to die.

Unfurl the flag of freedom
Salute your glorious sons,
They came from every walk of life
to fire and man the guns,
And through the skies across the seas
O'er many foreign lands,
They met the tyrant enemy
and smashed his heathen bands.

And when the war is over
when peace once more returns,
We'll think of those we left behind
as we watch the home fires burn,
We'll think of all those gallant lads
'Neath Burma's sweaty soil,
Who made the supreme sacrifice
the Japanese to foil.

From Dimapur to Kohima
through Imphals bloody plain,
The battle raged for many months
through heat and monsoon rain,
By Tamu's steaming jungle
along the Tiddim road,
And up the chocolate staircase
their gallant way they fought.

The road that crossed the frontier
leads on to Mandalay,
And their folks left for Tokio
we know no other way,
When the rising sun is set for good
and freedom's flag doth fly,
Salute the Fourteenth Army
They weren't afraid to die.

***126th Artillery Regiment***

## UNTITLED

I do not like the Germans
because they bombed our town
you see I was only ten
when they came to town
they dropped their bombs
they wrecked our homes
we never had a childhood because of them.
They must have been really bad men
my friends and I we could not play
because of the blackouts every day
we had to be home by five
we were told that was the only way we could stay alive
the blinds were on the windows
the lights were all put out
in case the German bombers
came back to start a fight.
I hate them every night.

***Cecilia Forbes***

## STRENGTH OF CARE

The third world countries
face many problems each hour
as widespread famine
is largely invisible to one's cue
as starvation is a
result of death.

UN do their best
for the children need care,
through many diseases they suffer despair,
as pain reflects
they are no longer aware
as most do need the strength of care.

Ethiopia conflicts with Eritrea
as millions appeal for help and aid,
as other countries may
reflect upon the UN.
Drought is a fact of life
where many people need
clean water, the third world
have no say, as they look up
through another bright day.

***Monica Rehill***

## FIELD SPORTS?

We have to cull them,
They all shout and all cry.
For if we don't to it and kill them
They will simply all die.
So they sit on their horses
And drink sherry and port
Before they set off on their horrible sport.
For they really think
They are kings of the hill.
Using hounds to hunt and to kill.
There sits each hunter high on his horse,
Digging his spurs in with terrible force.
Dragging at the metal in the poor horse's mouth,
There's something about them that is really uncouth,
Chasing the fox, the hart and the deer,
Until they collapse with heart-shaking fear.
A true hunter would need just some cord, and a knife,
But not those who think they are lords of all life,
Who sit on a horse, dragging the mouth
Digging their spurs in the poor horse's flanks
Then having killed, sit there and swanks.
Send them out with some cord and a knife,
See then if they can take an animal's life.

***Reginald T Dennis***

## A Harvest Of Shame!

From south to north
A tree falls and a typhoon calls.

From east to west
The wind sighs as the wildlife dies.

From pole to pole
The ice weeps yet the whole world sleeps.

From zone to zone
The earth burns; mankind never learns!

From age to age
Money sows as the sorrow flows.

And still . . .

We continue to guzzle at nature's breast
Leaving our children to reap the grim harvest!

***Susan M Billington***

## Family Of Man

Man has survived two thousand years,
the history books will shout.
Where is his comprehension
of what life is all about?

Technology has advanced the world,
a new era of the machine.
Souls imprisoned in a database,
accessible by a screen.

Nations clouded by iniquity,
allowed to soldier on.
Countless lives squandered.
We all recognise the wrong.

Innocence demands protection.
Pain must be relieved.
Colour is inconsequential
As age, gender and creed.

Created to be equal,
this evolving family of man.
Let our conscience be our guide,
empower us to understand.

***Karen Davies***

## Kosovo

The world out there
Is sinking into despair
Ills and carnage everywhere
In Kosovo.
Opening the floodgates
Hope has gone
And tomorrow never comes
No more sun and wars not won
Unseeing eyes,
Death from the skies.
Perhaps the soul lives on
But does life go on?
We know that 'Jesus wept'
And still weeps
For sorrows caused
And hate that reaps a battlefield,
No one escapes
The relentless passion
Of lives in despair, everywhere,
The burnt out flags
And no one to care?
A blackened sky
Where no birds sing
Why has hate and fury done this thing
In Kosovo.

***Joan Hands***

## My World

Conceived in the war
Born in liberty
A childhood of nature

Wandering across the moors
Walking to school
No one to harm you
They were the safe days

No television
No running water
No electricity
No fast foods

Remembering the oil lamps
Bathing in front of the fire
Outside to the loo
That was so cold in winter, frozen

What did I love most of all
The beautiful moors
I spent my childhood wandering
That feeling of being safe, secure

This was my world
A safe world of wonder.

***Carole A Cleverdon***

## BRAVE NEW WORLD

I looked in the mirror - and what did I see?
- My mother's face, staring at me,

'Peggy,' she said with a wistful tone,
'I have one wish, I don't want to moan,
But now that I have an overall view,
My ambition is to welcome the new!
To see the millennium come to a close,
And how the next one develops and grows.'

'Mam,' I replied with a positive sigh,
'You don't want to know how the world has gone by

'With everyone left on a slippery slope
Leading to nothing, no lightness, no hope!
Old people frightened - and young ones too
All from the acts of a horrible few.
Just down the street, and outside the door
See them a-gathering - hear their foul roar.

Batten the hatches, imprison your hope,
Live your life sadly, in darkness and mope!'

***Margaret Kellman***

## TSERING

I see the cold harsh reality staring;
Wishing! Wishing for the security
That we take for granted.
The warmth of happiness;
The sanitary of love;

And all she does is sit watching the day pass her by,
Her suffering slowly strangling every last breath of life.

But what of her life?

She is left to fend for herself;
To beg for every last scrap of food;

She is a face without recognition.
She is one name out of thousands.

She is one in a maze waiting to die;
To end her existence, her misery;

There is no fight left in her eyes;
She wishes for salvation,
And all she gets are scraps of half eaten food.

And day after day she sits in hope
That her prayers will be answered.

Yet day after day she sits and watches
The everyday people pass her by:
Glaring; jeering.

And as I stand here watching her indignantly,
I ask myself:
Who will take care of her?
Who will show her compassion?

Because she has nowhere left to turn!

***Marcus Tyler***

## World In Focus - In 2000

So much has happened on our planet
Affecting the balance - it is man that has done it!
There are so many cars with new roadways and extended towns -
Letting out exhaust fumes and aircraft seems to be polluting the air.
Ozone is killing the ultra-violet rays of the sun and causes cancer.
We also need smokeless zones - atomic rays and factory exhaust
cause sickness
Will there be a change in the millennium - to the folks on the planet?

Scientists predict that through the law of gravity
The stars - in time will disappear and then darkness -
The volcanic eruptions cause an effect on the sunlight with
the falling ash -
Heavy rainfall causing floods and people lose their homes -
We cannot change this, it is the environment - not man this time.

Society has changed as well, there is the closure of major industries!
Causing unemployment - these situations are fears but what
of our future?
New government? People are turning to crime for a living.
Can we help the people in the third world? The drought and the famine?
Has God bestowed such things upon us or is man the cause?
We are all expecting the advanced technology - the coming thing -
Let us go into 2000 perhaps with more faith, then we may have luck!
Affecting the balance of the planet, as yet we do not know!

***M E Smith***

## FIND A BETTER WAY

Fox hunting, form of cruelty, which makes me feel ashamed,
A sport which makes tempers rise and often become inflamed.
Such a terrible, prolonged way to cull my red brushed friend,
And which culminates in an awful death at the trail's end.

Then the horses are treated cruelly, that being their fate,
Because they've to travel wildly carrying human weights.
Dogs are treated badly, daily they are kept in a cage,
Allowed to take part in fox hunts when young, killed when they age.

One dog running against one fox, surely a fairer test,
Foxes to me are cute, for farmers nothing but a pest.
But there has to be a better, kinder, humane way,
Let us help keep foxes' numbers down and then let them stay.

***S Mullinger***

## REMEMBRANCE SUNDAY

A wreath of poppies at the cenotaph laid
At 11 not a sound
A nation's mourning is spectated

Knowing not why or for what
A finger and your country needs you
Yes, to die while the exalted hide

The crippled, medaled, sit on wheels
Would they have been better killed
Life's cruelty exampled perfectly

Each one a story of pain
Thoughts of death caress their brain
Turning to speak to a friend now slain

Gun in one hand, maybe a whistle
They climbed the ladder and ran
Shooting at, shot by, people they'd never meet

Running across a field of injured screams
Their dreams knew no peace
Heroes fit for homes

So many images of war amass
At a ceremony decrying its futility
The only time irony brings no smile

Onlookers applaud and fall silent
A veteran who can't clap cries
A veteran who can't hear remembers

The deathly silence, so uncomfortable
The hate that must fill their heads
The screams come flooding back

***Kenny Morrison***

## LONG WHITE SILK

One breathless summer afternoon,
when they were making peace in the Middle East,
and my wife, dressed in long white silk,
was lying on her lounger, beneath a mauve parasol,
sipping champagne,
I wandered off across the soft lawn,
towards the shrubbery.

There, on damp mulch, under a laurel bush,
I found a rabbit, or I should say, half a rabbit;
just its torn-off hind quarters,
and a slug of greyish green gut.
Beneath the clear blue sky,
in the summer sunshine,
I felt a little queasy, almost sick.

In spite of this I stayed,
and watched the gruesome sight unfold
of hordes of insects getting down to business,
wallowing in guts and entrails,
squabbling over matted fur and rotting flesh,
climbing up the creature's thigh,
gobbling their way to the top.

In the end, in sheer disgust, I left them to it,
wandered back and kissed her ladyship upon the cheek;
then, beneath the hot sun, while insects gorged themselves,
and politicians were making peace,
getting down to business in the Middle East,
we tried to settle once again,
the guest list for our daughter's wedding.

***A K S Shaw***

## INSANITY

They are dropping bombs on a country,
Raining death down from the air,
Have we not learnt any lessons,
There are people way down there.

A bomb cannot recognise,
If you are friend or foe,
So stop this bloody lunacy,
And give diplomacy another go.

We will make our world a graveyard,
Millions of crosses point to the skies,
Pause now and think, before it's too late,
Before one other person dies.

***Terry Sorby***

## Lament Of A Fox

The hunters in their bright red coats,
Astride their horses how they ride,
Their aim, is to catch me,
So I must find a place to hide.

But for me to hide, there is no place,
Their hounds, soon will get my scent,
Then over the fields they all chase me,
Until my breath is nearly spent.

To the hunters in their bright red coats,
It is a day of sport,
And triumphantly their horns will sound,
If by the hounds I'm caught.

I would like to know what I have done,
To be treated in this way,
I can't shout for help like a human can,
I can only try to run away.

So will someone, please do something,
To stop these people hunting me,
All I ask, as one of God's creatures is,
To live my life in peace and be free.

***Maud Eleanor Hobbs***

## OMAGH - (15.8.98)

As the people of Omagh scream out in their pain,
May the heads of their murderers who hear bow in shame!
And let Ireland unite in one cry from the heart;
'Let the killing fields cease, and pray God let peace start!'

***Elaine Dean***

## Pandora's Box

Pandora's Box was opened and I saw bad things in there;
As I stepped aside I watched as they flew through the air.
Earthquakes, floods and famine - illness, crime and war,
Homelessness and beatings like I'd never seen before.

Was I only dreaming? Were these really in my view?
Floating in the air, the earthly things I'd hoped weren't true?
But then, on television came the news that made me shake;
Kobe, in Japan, it said, had suffered an earthquake.

Worried families 'round the world, receiving news they'd dread
That four thousand people in that country, now were dead.
Yet, in the previous week there had been news of rain and mud
In Malibu, where there had been a great, traumatic flood.

Filmstars, from their homes had fled to find some 'dry' relief
From the water's menacing that struck, just like a thief.
Switching channels, I could see some scenes I'd watched before,
Chechnya and Russia were continuing to war.

Then government officials were asking folk like me
To give my clothes and toys to help the Bosnian charity.
Next, I read of wicked things - husbands beating wives,
Children caught up in the trap and fleeing for their lives.

Horrible diseases surgeons try to cure with blades;
Meningitis, cancer, and the blood disease called AIDS.
Animals, just battered, and left to starve, I see;
And people sleeping in the streets; no homes like you and me.

Such worrying and heartache, making people take the 'knocks'
Just who released the Evil that was in Pandora's Box?

***Doreen Pickett***

## VICTIM

Cold, icy silence and a fear-filled mind.
Pausing in full motion to clarify the scene
Coming off the cold night street into what was once a home
To meet disaster full in the face
With an utterly miserable, sinking heart.
We'd only just left a few hours before
With feelings of warmth for our fellow men,
Trusting in the worth of mankind,
And safety surrounding our very souls,
Been out there laughing with our friends,
Relaxing after the daytime toil.
Spending a few coins on ourselves,
Reminding us we are worthy too.
Only to come back to a scene like this.
A vicious, unnecessary, destructive crime,
A victim of the present time
That allows the criminal to survive,
The robber to feel a clever lad
And the victim to feel he's failed to foresee
The outcome of his trust in his fellows.
Made to feel as if he'd been chosen,
A victim of the criminal's taste.
Picked out from all the other mortals
And made to feel fully aware
That nothing keeps you immune from this.
Whoever you are, whatever you feel
The criminal is mercenary,
Protected by the powers that be.
Leaving you a victim of
The crime, the state and uncertainty.

***Joan E Blissett***

## Freedom

To climb lofty mountains breathing fresh air -
To gaze into heaven and know God is there.
To stand without fear - to see far and wide,
To run barefooted in a slow ebbing tide.
These are just dreams - for I am not free,
Hopes for my children the world cannot see.

I have lived too long by the bullet and gun,
My brothers and sisters no longer are one.
Colour and creed the decisions of man,
I do not believe that this was God's plan.
I fought for a cause, but I do not belong
To the crowds who chant a bloodthirsty song.

My children need peace for a better tomorrow,
So bury today with the tears and the sorrow.
Brothers and sisters look over the land,
Seek out the enemy and give them your hand.
They too are hungry and also feel pain,
Their fighting for freedom is now all in vain.

Enough of the blood and harrowing cry
Of young men who never needed to die.
Thirsty and tired - I am now growing old,
Freedom is precious, I do not need gold.
I return to the mountains to breathe the pure air,
I gaze into heaven - my freedom is there.

***Judy Thomas***

## Beliefs

I was raised on a farm, trained for nursing
While things changed all around us.
Some for the better, others for the worse.
The creation of clones worries me.
Does God really want us to rival him?
Most media news is awful, especially the wars
But we rarely learn what caused them.
As a child I cried 'Why?' when a lamb died,
As a nurse, 'Why?' for a baby to die.
Since my training days, improvements have fought
And conquered many a terminal disease.
But still we hear of faraway lands where
Starvation silences forever infants and adults alike.
Yet treatment far more simple than complex science
Would put an end to all this death and suffering.
People are at war, fighting for their children's lives,
Saying 'For chance to freedom' to kill for its delight
So many excuses for the centuries' battles and wars,
Declaring there must be 'One True Belief' for all.
God was worshipped in pre-Christian days,
Then bloody Crusades in Christ's name.
So many religions adhered to - their followers' way of life
Continued through so many centuries.
Buddhism, Judaism, Islam where Allah is God's name
And the Koran their blessed Book.
But, as in so many religions,
Women suffer disrespect.
So many strong beliefs
Which have so many malcontents!

***Tilla B Smith***

## The Three Rs

Reading between the lines
Of the 'riting on the wall -
Those from the middle classroom
Of conservative moralities
Need no longer nurture fears
About declining standards
And the emphasis of teaching
Not being based firmly on three Rs;
Anyone keen enough to get off his,
Or hers, will find that every
Urban inner-city curriculum
Has preached these lessons -
Together with the harsh realities -
For perhaps too many years,
And - not falling on deaf ears -
The message has been reaching
More students than was thought;
Now the 'rithmatic adds up
To tables being turned,
As well as being learned,
Because those who've fought
For better qualifications,
Being well-armed with grievances,
Have had enough of education,
And have graduated to the streets,
Spelling out in brown, as well as
Black and white, a new syllabus
Of violence based on four Rs: riot,
Retaliation, revenge and retribution.

***Derek J Pluck***

## POOLS OF PRAYER TEARS

Our screen is full of dying babies
And children forced to fight,
'It's awful dear, please pass the jam,'
And my aunt takes another bite.
I'm sick inside, really sick,
And ask what we can do,
'Get on with your tea and wipe your mouth,
Be thankful that it's not you.'

She grumbles that the milk's gone off,
Gets the paper to swat some flies;
Can't she see the suffering little ones,
With flies encrusting their eyes?
'Shall we send some money to that address
To help those people live?'
'They know nothing else, so there's no point.'
But I've decided to give.

I've prayed to God to help me know
What a kid like me can do,
He says 'You keep on trying Joe
And together we'll get through.
Your tears are forming pools of prayer
That will help to quench their thirst;
Keep showing the grown-ups what to do
Till they learn what matters first.'

Our class at school listened to me,
We've sent so many things there,
To try to help those little ones
And show how much we care.

***Ann Hulme***

## ADDICTION

Last night I had a dream so real it woke me with a fright.
'Twas all about a cigarette, but with no match to light!
I gave up smoking long ago to prove it could be done.
And now I have this great desire to have another one.

If I could only smoke just one my craving would be cured.
And you my dear would never know the deception you've endured.
Of all the people in the world that I must fool the most
'Tis you my lovely, caring wife . . . my soul's forever lost.

My health has gone and I must say goodbye forever dear.
We'll meet again some other day, on that I have no fear.
This sickness that will take my life has strengthened much this day.
So now my sweet angelic wife, a last request I pray.

Please give to me a candle light before my life is o'er,
'Tis now for breath that I must fight. I cannot cheat no more.
The only problem I have left is what to say to you.
When you catch me with my cigarette . . .
And find my sickness . . . 'tis just the flu!

***Harriett Turner***

## OUR CREATION

Will there be peace in our time?
That's something we don't know
Battles have been fought
And won centuries ago.
War brings devastation
Heartache and pain
Children are left orphans,
And their lives will never be the same,
Old buildings have been demolished
It's not a thing to do.
They have stood for centuries
And were our heritage too.
We don't want to
Build anymore roads
For dangerous drivers who
Don't bother with the highway code.
The floods, famine, and drought,
Is just nature's way.
We can't stop this from happening
No matter what we say
We have a lot of work to do
For the younger generation
The buildings will be our heritage
And also our creation.

***D Hardwick***

## Thinking

Do we ever really think
About the things we really need to
We spend half our lives fretting
About things that don't concern us
Do we need to get involved
With the subjects we don't believe in
Why do we like to hear our own opinions
Even if we don't understand the question

We open our mouths and hear a voice
Do we understand what we said
Let alone the question that was asked
Do we take the time to process the thought
That provoked the result we did not want

What kind of people are we
That thrive on the sorrow
And the pity of others
Have we listened to what they have said
Or are we too busy listening to our own opinions
To understand the needs of the land
We need to regress to understand
The law of life if you understand.

***Carol Williams***

## MISPLACED TRUST

The news we didn't want to come
and yet we knew it all along,
embedded in this world gone wrong:
She was too young to die alone.

So now the searchers trudge back home
to face the truth of what's been done
where innocence is rudely pricked
while satan's spoil's still on the run.

And why on earth the seed is sown
and how green have the rushes grown
and what has happened to the rain
to drown a little child's pain?

***Julian Collins***

## SCIENCE?

The scientist said with lifted brow,
There's work to be done, go to it now.
Forward looking, up to date
Forget the past it is too late.
We'll satisfy the needs of man
And give him all he wants - we can.
They thought they did and more than that
They fattened the thin and reduced the fat.
And still they did not rest content,
But following their realistic bent
Deprived man of his mind and soul
And poked statistics in the hole.

The computer said not why or how,
The PR man was called in now
To lead the masses by the nose -
'Where we lead he always goes.
Watch our science escalate,
Hurry now we cannot wait;
And if the parts we should dissect
The whole we cannot now respect.
If the bubble clutched is lost
We do not stop to count the cost.'
But oh I mourn the life we knew
When things weren't dead but lived and grew.

Scientific reason . . .
'Tis to my mind treason.

***G Poole***

## THE COUNTRYSIDE

Why not give the country
Its beauty, it once knew
*Or*, extend the towns in the area
And dig roads through and through

Why throw rubbish in the river
*To pollute this very way*
*And* give the countryside its meaning
The beauty, to this day

Why the pollution that collects in the sea
That once was clean and clear
Where holidaymakers love to swim
And play with the calm waves near

Why build on the countryside
Where once there was peace and quiet
Where birds like to fly and sing
*From early morn till night*

Why make the roads so large
To turn everything upside down
When the beauty laid around
In the country and the town

Why not let nature take its course
Where flowers bloom around
And the birds like to be so free
To chirp their sweetest sound

*Now the country seems overpowering*
While, strangers come over here for a place
More buildings on the landscape
Where once the farmers did plough their space

***Jean P McGovern***

## A World Of Opposites

One man's penny,
Another man's pound.
One man's noise,
Another man's sound.

One man's riches,
Another man's rags.
One man's feet,
Another man's Jags.

One man's friends,
Another man's foes.
One man's devils,
Another man's heroes.

One man's love,
Another man's hate.
One man's choice,
Another man's fate.

One man's own,
Another man's loan.
One man's need,
Another man's greed.

***Martin Short***

## UNTITLED

I sit in my own little domain
And feel no pain
Don't want to look at the world outside
Instead I choose to hide
What do I care if someone starves?
If someone gets shot?
I have my car and my mobile phone
I eat like a lord
And have a place to call my home
For the selfish actions of others
I could have peace
Do I want to give money?
Who's giving me it?
I throw away that which I do not want
Buy what I please
It is funny but just the other day someone said
That here on earth I am just another disease

I wonder what they meant?

***Maria Waters***

## RUSH HOUR

Arthritic caterpillar of the morning,
  where is your destiny?
Tortuous taxis for the traveller,
what progress have you made?
Standing, standing, creeping, standing,
snorting acrid smoke from every orifice.
Bathed in reflected red light,
a multi-eyed monster supposedly on the move.
Suddenly one metre of black tarmac appears,
an involuntary spasm judders from head to tail
causing segments of a once orderly body to leap forward
and gobble up the waiting black road.
The weary eyes flash in red anger, screaming -
*This is my territory, stand back. Stop!*

***Ian Garside***

## Born Free?

How free are the wild ones wand'ring the glade?
Blessed with nature's bounty - no need to be afraid;
Instinct to protect them and guide them what to eat;
With built-in protection, attackers to defeat;
Each one is born in its right habitat,
With all provided to its own format
So, what has gone wrong that so many we lose?
Many species endangered we hear on the news!

Why does man think that the Earth's his alone
To wield jurisdiction, and *all* he may own?
Robbing God's creatures of their daily needs;
Uprooting their shelter and sowing the seeds
Of destruction and suff'ring, famine, disease,
To bring a whole species on to its knees!
Not just for culling to keep balance right,
But to satiate greed, they put reason to flight!

Man best watch out, lest his own fate he seals;
Not considering others, despite appeals,
Brings repercussions not easy to halt;
In learning our lesson and repenting our fault,
We may find it's too late to make amends
And stay destruction to reverse the trends;
We must show compassion, and know our place
In the animal kingdom, choose what our race.

Though man sees himself as master supreme,
With powers to reason and talent to scheme,
It behoves to respect *all* creatures' worth,
And acknowledge their value and part on this Earth;
For, we all have our part to play in the scheme -
To think we are owners, is a foolish man's dream!

***Bee Wickens***

## What Is The Answer?

Help! Halt the world, we need to escape;
Flee from disasters, disease and mistakes.
Yet leaving this world in a sorry state,
   is condemning others to an even worse fate.

We've misused resources, seeking for power;
Done countless damage, hour after hour;
Harboured our grudges, repossessions and land,
   festering new wars on every hand.

Then what is the answer, stay and fight?
Wrestle and grapple for what we think right;
Tool ourselves up with the latest device,
   and to hell with consequence, no matter the price?

Love could be the answer; love and not hate
Throughout the whole world, before it's too late.
Begin with the children, and integrate
   through some common language with which to relate.

Share our resources; share all our skills,
Pulling together to cure the world's ills.
A century it may take or a millennium . . .
   but for a world worth saving, it must be done.

***Cynthia Smith***

## Deliver Us From Evil

If I kill my unborn
Knowingly,
Legally,
Dispose of my child
In this culture of death,
And endorse his last breath.
And because of the anguish
This pregnancy brought,
Society taught me
My interests first -
Affliction get rid of;
Encumbrance abort,
When I am a burden,
Mentally,
Socially;
Old age deprives me
Of reason and health,
Because of the anguish
To my family *I've* brought,
Society taught them
*Their* interests first -
Affliction get rid of;
Encumbrance abort,
Then I won't complain if
Knowingly,
Legally,
*They* take my life
In this culture of death,
They endorse *my* last breath.

***I Munro***

## Good Thoughts

Life can be so wonderful
Getting on the right track
Keeping thyself cool
Keeping the mind intact
Authors of long ago
Realised such a life
It keeps one from unfound woe
And one realises less strife

Good to have folk around you
But does not bring contentment
There are folk of a few
Who will surely comment
If one looks to their need
With 'good thoughts' in the mind
This brings goodwill and prestige
As one will always find

If one is kind to another
And not receiving respect
Altho' good to be together
Thou need not feel reject
Keeping within the 'laws of nature'
Life is more steady
You may rest assured
Which other folk wish to be.

***Josephine Foreman***

## Make-Up Lady

You used make-up
so you were asking for it
right?

You didn't even get your face
the other side of the camera
just a foot sticking out of the rubble

Soldiers die
it's accepted (if not acceptable)
but your crime was to paint the faces
and cover the sweat
of those who stood in the glare
of more than studio lights.

You thought we'd never come for you
but we did. We had to.
That's what our spokesman said
without a blush.
Maybe we have make-up ladies too.

And now colour-fast will no longer hide
the shame I feel
nor cover the crimes of national pride.

***Henry Birtley***

## TOWARDS 2000

Is this it? Can this be so?
A world still at war
Still full of woe

Here we are on the brink of what?
Flood and drought
Another filthy ethnic plot
Nothing learnt
Another village burnt.

Did compassion creep in?
Greed on the run
It seems not yet
Power's a better bet
Infamy's more fun

Road rage, air rage, shop rage, what rage!
Band aid, sport aid, what aid?
Poverty still rife
Turmoil and strife
The world keeps spinning
But nobody seems to be winning
Have we left it too late?
Do we deserve to survive?
Remember this date if you're still alive.

***M Yockney***

## LOST DREAMS

I sat with students in the sixties
Listening to their dreams,
Of love and peace, and food for all,
How long ago it seems,

That we held hands across the world,
And faith from shore to shore,
Combined in ocean strength to stem
The tide of Vietnam war.

What hope of future's free from fear
And hunger did we keep,
While lullabies of 'We shall overcome'
Sent babes to sleep.

And now we've wakened from our dreams,
And babes have grown to find
A world of plagues, and want and war,
Injustice of all kind.

God, did I let those children down,
That black boy on TV,
That while I sit in comfort
Let his hungry eyes haunt me?

Did I not keep a watch on those
Who thrive on human prey?
What principles of equal truth
And love did I betray?

***Janette Valentine***

## The Searchers

Long after the picture has gone
the haunting scene lingers on.
Deep feelings come to mind,
pity for the survivors left behind,
with tearless eyes, so utterly sad,
looking for a dear one, missing - dead.

In the aftermath of ethnic cleansing,
they follow the research team, clinging
to the hope of finding a dear one's body
in the mass grave of many 'nobodies'
furtively buried after execution,
with cruel haste, uncaring, no emotion.

Some scantily attired, some pitifully bare,
with no name, not a clue anywhere.
After digging, the experts analyse
bones and remains to recognise
gender, age, a gruesome task,
for human dignity it is a must.

The survivors waiting day after day
to identify a loved one in some way.
A ring, a cross, a chain or some other
property of a daughter, a wife, a mother.
After a while, big, small moulds
are left, testimony of atrocities untold.

***Licia Johnston***

## CHILDREN EVERYWHERE

Children are important to the human chain,
Yet many suffer hardship, degradation and pain.

Each one of us once a child, of course that is a fact,
Wouldn't it be wonderful if we could make a pact
That children in need, be a thing of the past -
Before that could happen, a lot of help needed, a lot to ask . . .

I recall during the war, to save our children
They were sent to strange lands,
To escape from Hitler's evil hands,
In every communication we had to beware -
Every sunset a quiet voice sang 'Goodnight children everywhere'

Where there is greed, men grasping for power,
Using money for guns their people to cower,
Their land is laid waste, the innocent flee -
'Did the children hear the Lord say 'Come unto me'?'

Will the little ones wither before they can flower?
We must stop the wicked ones wrongly using their power -

We must see that the money so generously sent
Is used to help people, not on guns spent.
I do not know how this can be done,
But until we can do it, the war to save the children can never be won . . .

***D E Jones***

## People Versus . . .

Everything is so simple, and so free, for all of everyone, but me.

Why cannot I find a hidden place, something so far away?
To escape the earth's strangled forces and go to my place of serenity.
My home.

Maddening world, everyone rushing by,
So hard to find a simple place to hide.

I want to be alone, I want to be free. I need to find the place my soul,
My heart needs.

Love is not as strong, as a strong-willed head and heart of stone.
How I wish to be a someone, of my own.

Whims and wants, indulgence, greed. Selfish pleas.
Why do we keep on fighting for the things it's hard to have?
Dreams are just a fantasy.

Pacing, there I am, frustrated all the time. How no one will ever listen,
To that I just want peace of mind.

Why does no one listen? What do I have to prove?
Do I have to force attention, or is that just a word?

Is the world just made up, of pointless words?

***Fiona E E Pearce***

## Millennium - Kampala Style

Charred and contorted bodies smoulder in the aftermath,
Stinking the burnt-out shell of a makeshift church.
A child's remains, couched foetus-like,
Seeps amongst the ashes of humanity. Debris into dust.
Twisted arms outstretched, each corpse cries with awful grin
Its plea for help,
With head awry, seared and bald.
Vacant, sooty, steaming sockets hint the untold agony
Each mirror of each soul had once displayed.
Eyes now extinct. Ashes to dust.
Hundreds in mass suicide.
An obscure cult they joined,
'Movement for the Restoration of the Ten Commands of God'.
Unrestored, 'Thou Shalt Not Kill'.
Children partied, drank soft drinks and bade goodbye
To neighbours, friends and families.
The Virgin Mary promised them salvation
With unhindered passage straight to Heaven.
Joyfully each one ran headlong to the lion's den.
To murder foul.
Door locked; window boarded up and nailed and torched.
'Suffer little children.'
Screaming piteously to no avail, they did just that.

***Ann Bryce***

## Why We Should Remember

The celebration of D-day on television,
Made me wonder if we should
Keep remembering every year.
If it does any real good.

It is fifty years ago it happened.
Would it be better to forget?
But when I looked at the rows
Of graves, can we forget it yet?

They were so white and spotless,
All in lines so straight and true.
So many hundreds of young men
Who died for me and you.

So many mothers and sweethearts,
Would see their sons and lovers no more.
So many sons and daughters
Never see their father come in the door.

Then there were the ones left behind,
They didn't have an easy life.
There was rationing and bombing.
Deaths and injuries were rife.

Evacuees were sent away from home.
Separated from their mothers.
Families were split up.
Sisters leaving brothers.

So we must keep on remembering,
Long after the old soldiers are dead.
And never to let it happen again.
We must always try to talk instead.

***Margaret C Rae***

## WAR

May those that survived,
Have memories that linger long.
As tomorrow no one will remember,
But those that were there.

***Ian Fisher***

## THE MASTER PLAN

God must have had a reason to make each of us
And everything that breathes and has a soul
For, quite apart from 'living' and 'survival' laws,
I'm sure we have a more *specific* role.

Not each of us is perfect and can help ourselves
So a large proportion helps his fellow man;
That is their task - fulfilling needs of lesser folk
And helping every day just where they can.

In man, God planted seeds of good and bad.
In some, the sweeter seed is left to die
Through deprivation; ignorance; so *many* things -
(Maybe survival stakes just got too high!)

Yet - sadly - there are those who live just for themselves
To 'get', 'get' 'get' - to hell with anyone
Who hasn't got the latest in just everything
Creative man has made beneath His sun . . .

But, there are thousands more that God has given gifts
To entertain - to make us smile and say:
'Life's not so bad - now that I've laughed it's made me strong
And I can live to fight another day.'

Still, out of what is left there's surely got to be
A fairly large proportion - good and strong -
Who have the expertise, and who can point the way
To those among us who have got it wrong.

If this scattered power is harnessed, and the caring ones
Together make a force for unity
Then 'His master plan' for each lost soul can operate -
Designed for *all* - it's *Christianity* . . .

***Hannah Yates***

## War Remembered

Innocence
Take precedence,
With enemy near,
They run in fear.
All this madness,
Terror, sadness,
Young and old,
Brave and bold,
Crazed dictator,
People hater.
End their sorrow,
Bring joy tomorrow.
They leave their homes,
The hills they roam,
Left with nothing,
No home or belongings.
Death was there,
In Bosnia.
Help was nigh,
From do or die,
Heroes all,
Answered the call,
To end the fear,
In Bosnia.

***Anne Marie Birley***

## FATE

Too many words have been spoken,
too much time and effort spent.
Without the horrors of war,
man can never be content.

He builds his lethal weapons,
more complex across the years.
Never thinking of the destruction,
without seeing the children's tears.

War is just another crime,
a sickness spread by the human race.
Men can always make excuses,
the truth they will never face.

The greed, and the stupidity,
one day will kill us all.
But until the final day,
the bombs will always fall.

*M A Challis*

## Never Call It Sport

We're put upon this earth
To nurture and to care
For everything that's here
And creatures everywhere.

We feed and pat our dogs,
Stroke cats so lovingly.
The beauty of a fox
Is there for all to see.

Most humans eat their sheep
And feast on chicken too.
The fox is doing just
What humans always do.

And who can judge their worth,
To die or to let live?
The foxes kill and eat
In order to survive.

To hunters in red coats
It's just a good day's ride
But think how he must feel.
The fox is terrified.

Pursued across the fields
Until by hounds he's caught.
He's ripped to pieces then
So *never* call it sport.

***Felicity Fonteyn***

## UNTITLED

beggars out
for the passing eyes
look on it pity
no money can buy back his limbs
he now displays for a living
stalls of the poor
porn
buttons
combs
sell themselves for a penny or more
you close your eyes of what you see
poverty
living on their knees
begging
living in the streets
teenage girls walking the street
to make ends meet
tourist eyes search
for the pretty ladies on poverty's beat
eyes of lust
fantasy
of what money can do
on poverty's streets
where the money reeks
money the language everyone speaks

***Terrance A Williams***

## I'VE JUST WATCHED THE NEWS

Will this pain in my heart ever go away
I've just watched the news, so sad today
Racism is the root, it seems to be
We are all the same, why can't they see

God is our Father, he loves us all
Black, brown or white, big or small
He gave us this planet to make a life
To live in harmony, not cause all this strife

I pray for peace to reign everywhere
For freedom of spirit, not bogged down by fear
Clothes for warmth and enough food to eat
Not to be frightened by every stranger we meet

***Patricia Mackie***

## Time Is Not My Enemy

*Son* of *sorrow* you're my *friend*
With open arms the truth will be
Come to me we'll see the end
For time is not my enemy

*Tomorrow* I will close my eyes
With you I shall be free
To leave my footprints in the skies
And ride on waves of ecstasy

In search of truth I lost the cause
My heart was open as the seas
Came first disease then came the wars
They're written in the centuries

Bring to me your symphony
Your spirit outlives death
I stroll your realms of sanctuary
As the earth exalts its breath

Return to me tranquillity
Your rivers and your forests
The open plains, the screaming sea
Make love in freedom endlessly
This place where pleasure manifests
Where time is not my enemy.

***Sparky***

## DISASTER STRIKES

Shut cellar door
drop to the floor
then I went for bombers to leave.
No need to hide
I rush outside,
for hours I cried and now I grieve.

I stand alone
no place to roam.
A mass of moans hangs everywhere.
Don't dare to speak.
My body weak.
The town so bleak and greatly bare.

Onward I go
shuffles so slow.
My spirit low, I hang my head.
A blazing ball.
No need to call -
I know that all around are dead.

Tears in my eye
I walk on by.
The midnight sky is filled with light.
Myself I'll fend,
my heart might mend.
Disastrous end in just one night.

***Kathryn Seymour***

## World In Crisis

World in crisis, bruised by vices sore by force by man's own cause
Rocks the face of the earth with his inventions,
Cause tension with more sickness to mention.
Diseases slow healing with more pain than one can mention
With most deaths caused by inventions
Technology is another one to mention
The tensions of man's own preventions
Mass productions cause destruction to the lives of the infants
Feeding toxins through the blood stream of one's own being
And feeling the strain while it works through the veins
Causing horror and pain, oh what a shame
Caused by fame with more money than brains
Oh what a pain.

***Sonia Bowen***

## HEARTACHES OF MODERN DAYS

Today there seems more heartache,
Some of which nature does make,
Shown on television, it comes loud and clear,
Though we long for a better world,
There is always lots of fear:

There are land slides and floods,
And the dreaded hurricanes,
Leaving many without a home,
Then they have to wander and roam:

This is when you realise . . .
Others on Earth are your brother,
We always need each other by our side,
Regardless of creed or colour:

Remember those who suffer,
In lots and many ways . . .
All can find you if you know of care,
So too, are willing to share:

You young ones of today,
Remember there are others who will come,
In later dates, your children,
Pull yourselves together, in this world:

I hope things will be better . . .
*God bless you all*, no matter where or who,
May this planet earth see love to share,
And future generations value its *worth*.

***Anita M Slattery***

## Clear The Debris

What should a man of God teach?
Love thy neighbour.
Toleration in all things.
Listen to what others have to say.
Peace . . . turn the other cheek.
No eye for an eye to pay.
Violence in voice or act to abhor.
Inciting others will bring sin on its wings.

What have they in Ireland?
A religious leader who preaches
The Devil's mandate.
How can peace be consolidated
With bigots shouting whilst love loses.
Their cries, by news agencies encouraged,
When thugs, bullies and murderers planned
The end of children's lives with hate.

Where are the church officials?
Why don't they act
Against those clergy who preach
Contrary to the teachings of 'the Book' given?
Where is the desire to impeach
Those rogue elements . . . to have them sacked
From the pulpit they have forsaken
And blasphemed with the Devil's talk.

***Terry Baldwin***

## POLLUTION - HOPE FADES

The car of yesterday and of today
Have something in common. Which leads me to say
If they had been thought of tomorrow, no doubt,
No pollution the call. It must produce nought.

With carbon monoxide a suicide's dream.
And bodies that rust lying close to a stream.
There's nothing we like, with all its congestion,
Than a dose of lead with our digestion.

The nuclear age was to have been a great boon.
Cheap electricity for all quite soon.
But the contamination unseen brings fears
When they have to be stored for thousands of years.

It's all very safe. Nothing can happen here.
Overlook any scare in the States, so we hear.
Chernobyl is just a flash in the pan.
But the land is not safe o'er which sheep once ran.

In olden times the farmers used their lands
With love and care. Rotating fields in bands.
Now they ask for higher yields from seeds they sow.
Artificial fertilisers make them grow.

The concentrations they pour on create
The growth that's wanted. It soon may be too late
To stop the poisoning of our water clear.
No life to see in river, stream I fear.

This land of ours, once green and pure of air,
Writhes in agony. Attacked by things man made.
To count the cost to heal this ancient lair
Is naught against the search in space. Hopes fade.

***Maureen Baldwin***

## The Red Sea

Cold and obscenely
They twist the sharpened knife
And paint the blue sea red.

Beautiful creature
How could they butcher you
And show you no mercy?

Tortured cries
Fill up empty skies
From your orphaned young.

Callous and cruel
Men with stained hands
Sit and tell small jokes
As they count their blooded money.

***Deborah L Wilson***

## JUST A LOOK

To stop and look at this world
Ever moving, always growing
To not put a stop on nature changing
Never undo what it's doing
And never to try and erase the start
If we look back at where it started
We'll see how at first it was meant to be
All the delicates of real beauty
And an innocent image of you and me
Then why do we harm this decor
And what should make us want to fill
If ever there was a good enough reason
The victim would have still been crushed in the mill.

***Naomi Elisa Price***

## Human

If truth can come from the heart,
And if life can imitate the art,
If you can change your tune,
And if the earth can circle the moon,
If you can turn on your heels,
And if a hot Sunday roast appeals,
If you can be happy and smile,
And if the wars could stop for a while,
If your worries can make you laugh,
And if your deficits were cut in half
If we all can be good to each other,
And if we talk to our father and mother,
If dreams could all become real,
And if emotions will let you feel,
If we all came together to pray,
And if we make that a joyous day,
If we all looked up to the sky,
And if it brought a tear to your eye,
We realise there is no more pain,
And we could all be human again.

***Jamie Barnes***

## The Ivory Tower

The ivory tower, our elephant friend
He roams across the land
A rifle fires, he falls down
He cries for help and hits the sand

What does he think as he lies in pain
Why do men cut off his tusks
He cries and you can see his tears
In fear of men for money lusts

They are a social family beast
And play their trumpets when they can
The leader he will stand his ground
And defend them from greedy man.

We can not let this carry on
Taking precious lives like this
Remove all ivory from all sales
Let them live a life of bliss

When such men meet our dear Lord
When their lives draw to an end
Will he forgive and tell them all
The elephant is our friend

***A F Mace***

## NEVER ENDING

Independence . . . independence,
Lingering convictions fester and simmer,
Struggles continually in ascendance,
Undeclared yet grim and grimmer.

The highjacked plane, the station bomb,
Intestines spew from gory lesions.
History speaking with forked tongue,
Instilling hatred over reasons.

Blackmail, threats and hostage taking,
Suicidal tactics solicit applause,
From those, especially money-making,
Supplying weaponry for the cause.

Demands unchanging, no verbosity,
Negotiation not a mention,
Delivered between each atrocity,
Humanism's circumvention.

Support available near and far,
Righteousness believed on their side,
Not in their thought-box repertoire,
Could recognition's fight not be God inspired.

In Europe we seem to have turned a page,
As politicians' numbers grow to lengths absurd,
Togetherness, amalgamation is all the rage,
Independence the casualty . . . now a dirty word.

Preferable or not only time will say,
But those never silent bands of war,
Which permanently takes ones breath away,
Could play the lament for us once more.

***Frank Valentine***

## WAR

Once more into the breach dear chums,
Hear the sound of thundering guns,
Fall to work, fall in air, fall wherever earth is gone.
Shoot and pummel in the ground, fighting,
Climb and shout and fall and drown, fighting,
Hiding, running, screaming, deserting,
Soldiers hunting, finding, searching,
Rain of bullets, breeze of fire, stomping feet,
Frostbite, burns, cold and hotness meet,
Crushing, pushing, stuffing down,
Stuffing, falling, crumbling down,
Drowning, dying, falling, looking for the enemy,
Snow driving, the wind's harsh searching gentility,
Jumping, charging, fear has a home,
Jumping, charging, each to his own,
Run for your death, run for the end,
Fight for your country, fight for your kin,
Hoping another will never begin,
Dragging home, crawling, drowning, swimming,
The screen is up, your dying film,
Lead the way, halt and die,
Run and run and run and run and die.

***Julie Ann Evans***

## The Killer

The farmwife bustled across the yard to shut up her hens for the night.
Fifty fat birds which laid fine eggs to sell -
She knew every one by sight.
But when she went in and slept sound in her room
Came the evil red killer - the harbinger of doom.
All fifty he slew, biting off each one's head;
Only for fun - not to eat - and left every one dead.

The young ewe groaned as she strained to bring forth
The lamb - her firstborn child -
On the bare hillside in the streaming wet,
With the stormwind raging wild.
Birth came at last as she panted for breath,
Then nuzzled the lamb by her side,
But she dared not rest, for the killer she saw,
With his eyes fastened on her pride.
Forward he came, belly low to the ground,
And his slavering jaws were wide,
And the tired ewe stood in front of her lamb
To give it some place to hide.
In vain the weary mother sheep tried to beat him off
As she smelt his vile scent,
But he dodged with ease, and killed her babe;
Left it lying there, and went.

Town people who say hunting's cruel to the fox
Should be told what we countryfolk know -
He's a stinking killer, who murders for sport,
And mercy he never will show.

***Marjorie Piggins***

## A Balkan Village

Always obsessively the cold sky
Above the round searchlight, with clean lines
Always mounted on the roof of the bungalow.
Gives strength to the perception of the flow,
Around the town, of obsessive detail
Here beneath the mountainside
Where the houses nestle near the stream.
  Note the plain on the other side seems
Under an different cold sky at this epoch . . .

***Michael Courtney Soper***

## Refugees

Refugees . . . A long winding trail
Like ants on the move.
Unending.
Towards a far horizon and the unknown.
Leaving in their wake
Burning homes. Menfolk killed. Rape.

Refugees are all the same
Whichever century or whatever race they're from.
A human convoy of pathetic bundles,
Some on foot,
Others carried on makeshift handcarts.
Ponies. Tractors. Cars.

Refugees. Victims of ethnic cleansing.
Destination and future
Uncertain.
Age peers out with unseeing eyes at the changing scene,
And children, the innocents, gaze in silent terror
Through hollowed eyes that have seen too much.

Refugees. And still they come.
Over mountains. Through forests. Rivers.
In strange fields babies are born, the sick and elderly die
And are laid to rest in shallow graves.
How many miles to Babylon?
Fatigue. Hunger. Thirst.

Refugees. Overcrowded camps where birds no longer sing.
Only the wails of those mourning their dead
And the cries of lost children
Punctuate the silence.
Barren earth. Filth. Squalor. Mud.
My God, my God, why hast thou forsaken me?

***Rosina Winiarski***

## DEATH OF A PRINCESS

Scent of hypocrisy fills the air,<br>
Rampant hysteria everywhere,<br>
Strangers with intimate stories to tell,<br>
Traders with oceans of flowers to sell,<br>
Guilt seeking scapegoats to shoulder the blame,<br>
Inadequates seeking their moment of fame,<br>
Conjured illusions and fairy tale dreams,<br>
Nothing is ever at all like it seems.

Rodent reporters inciting the crowd,<br>
Voicing opinions in ignorance proud,<br>
Soap-opera attitudes, applewoman minds,<br>
Sentiment flourishes as reason unwinds.<br>
World weary royals produced to perform,<br>
Flag lowering, hand pressing, caught in a storm,<br>
Where mobs can dictate and the media connive<br>
What damage is done to those who survive?

Reason retreats, unreality rules<br>
For suddenly this is the kingdom of fools

***Paddy Lease***

## OUR HOPES

Our hopes are dashed, high hopes sunken to no hope.
Disappointments all around.
Our parenting was to be so skilled and graded.
To be the best ever.
Oh the excitement of your birth, with the pleasure
In your first steps, all leading to the way it should.
Your looks, the manner with natural easy nature.
Eyes of envy were often glanced.
A recent memory loss was the evil eye that did it.
Planned future out of reach, the steps that went
Upwards, had an awkward twist.
You found solace from an synthetic mixture
This is the tricky spot.
Great advice from the wisest in our land, 'cast them out'.
This we did and nearly lost them.
Compared to this, memory loss sounds as meryth.
We cast him out, he nearly died.
My A1 ok, a little jittery . . . still the brightest
In the bunch.'
Accepting this was hard for us and harder still for him.
Admitting, meaning talking helped, then others spoke
Said of their hell that came through it.
Others didn't 'dead in a loo'.
Accepting, dealing with it, caring seems to be
The most productive that I find as I'm still 'in there'.

***Margaret Gleeson Spanos***

## Who Am I?

How can I say anything as I lay here warm in my bed
Staring at the ceiling that covers my head?
How can I whine about my life of misery and boredom
When I smell the food I have just cooked?
How can I complain about not having any fun
As I watched Americans parade on my digital TV?

Who am I to say that there is something that everyone else can do
When I do nothing myself?
Who am I to whine about the waste of public resources
When I am wasting them myself?

I don't live in the real world of suffer to live
I live in a country where all the priorities are wrong
I live in a country that doesn't know extremes
'A little of what you fancy does you good'
But kills your sensibilities

Even when nature throws her very worst at the people outside
of our illustrious nation
Still they dance and sing and thank God for what they do have
When we are looking out of the window and moaning about the
rain and taxes.

***Rebecca Bennett***

## UNTITLED

Whilst we lament the law and the trial of justice,
Victims lie bleeding;

Whilst the deities of evil endeavour to pervade
Their fantasies misleading;

And whilst propagating wolves stand howling their delusions,

Their targets are yielding.

***Anita-Marie Kilbourne***

## The Queen Mother's Birthday

A wonderful day, a cloudless sky,
For the apple in the nation's eye
A lifetime of service spent unselfishly
Being one of love, and loyalty

Millions of subjects, young and old
Determined to see the story unfold
A woman of beauty and quiet strength
Led the nation in peace, and content

This special day celebrates one hundred years
An example to all can dispel any fears
A future to follow, in her loyal stead
Is assured success, from the example, she led

Alone she reigned with strength and courage
Welcoming the cheers, and wishes of all
With her family around her for support
Her happiness shines through from her court

The cavalcade, presenting all those years
Of many charities she supports, give cheers
The pageant, music, colours, and many displays
Give thanks to her reign, for many more days

There she stands, elegant, in soft shell pink
A ready smile and a wave to link
The colourful parade of all those years
An achievement deserving all those cheers.

***C King***

## God Forsaken!

Life's grand the day - in every way;
the sun beeks doon wi high-temp heat;
the gairden's fu o' flooers an' fruit
an' as a say, it's grand the day; the taste is sweet!
But somewhere, monie miles frae here
it's nae that verra pleasant,
fowks live an' dee, aye under threat
for poet, wife or peasant.
Man's inhumanity to man
an' woman tae, for aa that
is close tae haund in terror's rule
while life aa roond's a death trap.
The dule an' wae that come thur way
is nae muckle tae thur likin' -
sae spare a thocht for man an' baste
beset aa roond by fighten'
an' ken yeir fortune, guid or bad
ti tak - thur nae escapin'!
Thur some o' us weel pleased the day -
but ithers - God forsaken!

***Andrew A Duncan***